What the fuck is my password.

Date:_____

Website:_____

Username:_____

Password:_____

Notes:_____

_____

_____

Date:_____

Website:_____

Username:_____

Password:_____

Notes:_____

_____

_____

Date:_____

Website:_____

Username:_____

Password:_____

Notes:_____

_____

_____

Date:_____

Website:_____

Username:_____

Password:_____

Notes:_____

_____

_____

Date:_____

Website:_____

Username:_____

Password:_____

Notes:_____

_____

_____

Date:_____

Website:_____

Username:_____

Password:_____

Notes:_____

_____

_____

Date:_____

Website:_____

Username:_____

Password:_____

Notes:_____

_____

_____

Date:_____

Website:_____

Username:_____

Password:_____

Notes:_____

_____

_____

Date:_____

Website:_____

Username:_____

Password:_____

Notes:_____

_____

_____

Date:_____

Website:_____

Username:_____

Password:_____

Notes:_____

_____

_____

Date:_____

Website:_____

Username:_____

Password:_____

Notes:_____

_____

_____

Date:_____

Website:_____

Username:_____

Password:_____

Notes:_____

_____

_____

Date:_____

Website:_____

Username:_____

Password:_____

Notes:_____

_____

_____

Date:_____

Website:_____

Username:_____

Password:_____

Notes:_____

_____

_____

Date:_____

Website:_____

Username:_____

Password:_____

Notes:_____

_____

_____

Date:_____

Website:_____

Username:_____

Password:_____

Notes:_____

_____

_____

Date:_____

Website:_____

Username:_____

Password:_____

Notes:_____

_____

_____

Date:_____

Website:_____

Username:_____

Password:_____

Notes:_____

_____

_____

Date:_____

Website:_____

Username:_____

Password:_____

Notes:_____

_____

_____

Date:_____

Website:_____

Username:_____

Password:_____

Notes:_____

_____

_____

Date:_____

Website:_____

Username:_____

Password:_____

Notes:_____

_____

_____

Date:_____

Website:_____

Username:_____

Password:_____

Notes:_____

_____

_____

Date:_____

Website:_____

Username:_____

Password:_____

Notes:_____

_____

_____

Date:_____

Website:_____

Username:_____

Password:_____

Notes:_____

_____

_____

Date:_____

Website:_____

Username:_____

Password:_____

Notes:_____

_____

_____

Date:_____

Website:_____

Username:_____

Password:_____

Notes:_____

_____

_____

Date:_____

Website:_____

Username:_____

Password:_____

Notes:_____

_____

_____

Date:_____

Website:_____

Username:_____

Password:_____

Notes:_____

_____

_____

Date:_____

Website:_____

Username:_____

Password:_____

Notes:_____

_____

_____

Date:_____

Website:_____

Username:_____

Password:_____

Notes:_____

_____

_____

Date:_____

Website:_____

Username:_____

Password:_____

Notes:_____

_____

_____

Date:_____

Website:_____

Username:_____

Password:_____

Notes:_____

_____

_____

Date:_____

Website:_____

Username:_____

Password:_____

Notes:_____

_____

_____

Date:_____

Website:_____

Username:_____

Password:_____

Notes:_____

_____

_____

Date:_____

Website:_____

Username:_____

Password:_____

Notes:_____

_____

_____

Date:_____

Website:_____

Username:_____

Password:_____

Notes:_____

_____

_____

Date:_____

Website:_____

Username:_____

Password:_____

Notes:_____

_____

_____

Date:_____

Website:_____

Username:_____

Password:_____

Notes:_____

_____

_____

Date:_____

Website:_____

Username:_____

Password:_____

Notes:_____

_____

_____

Date:_____

Website:_____

Username:_____

Password:_____

Notes:_____

_____

_____

Date:_____

Website:_____

Username:_____

Password:_____

Notes:_____

_____

_____

Date:_____

Website:_____

Username:_____

Password:_____

Notes:_____

_____

_____

Date:_____

Website:_____

Username:_____

Password:_____

Notes:_____

_____

_____

Date:_____

Website:_____

Username:_____

Password:_____

Notes:_____

_____

_____

Date:_____

Website:_____

Username:_____

Password:_____

Notes:_____

_____

_____

Date:_____

Website:_____

Username:_____

Password:_____

Notes:_____

_____

_____

Date:_____

Website:_____

Username:_____

Password:_____

Notes:_____

_____

_____

Date:_____

Website:_____

Username:_____

Password:_____

Notes:_____

_____

_____

Date:_____

Website:_____

Username:_____

Password:_____

Notes:_____

_____

_____

Date:_____

Website:_____

Username:_____

Password:_____

Notes:_____

_____

_____

Date:_____

Website:_____

Username:_____

Password:_____

Notes:_____

_____

_____

Date:_____

Website:_____

Username:_____

Password:_____

Notes:_____

_____

_____

Date:_____

Website:_____

Username:_____

Password:_____

Notes:_____

_____

_____

Date:_____

Website:_____

Username:_____

Password:_____

Notes:_____

_____

_____

Date:_____

Website:_____

Username:_____

Password:_____

Notes:_____

_____

_____

Date:_____

Website:_____

Username:_____

Password:_____

Notes:_____

_____

_____

Date:_____

Website:_____

Username:_____

Password:_____

Notes:_____

_____

_____

Date:_____

Website:_____

Username:_____

Password:_____

Notes:_____

_____

_____

Date:_____

Website:_____

Username:_____

Password:_____

Notes:_____

_____

_____

Date:_____

Website:_____

Username:_____

Password:_____

Notes:_____

_____

_____

Date:_____

Website:_____

Username:_____

Password:_____

Notes:_____

_____

_____

Date:_____

Website:_____

Username:_____

Password:_____

Notes:_____

_____

_____

Date:_____

Website:_____

Username:_____

Password:_____

Notes:_____

_____

_____

Date:_____

Website:_____

Username:_____

Password:_____

Notes:_____

_____

_____

Date:_____

Website:_____

Username:_____

Password:_____

Notes:_____

_____

_____

Date:_____

Website:_____

Username:_____

Password:_____

Notes:_____

_____

_____

Date:_____

Website:_____

Username:_____

Password:_____

Notes:_____

_____

_____

Date:_____

Website:_____

Username:_____

Password:_____

Notes:_____

_____

_____

Date:_____

Website:_____

Username:_____

Password:_____

Notes:_____

_____

_____

Date:_____

Website:_____

Username:_____

Password:_____

Notes:_____

_____

_____

Date:_____

Website:_____

Username:_____

Password:_____

Notes:_____

_____

_____

Date:_____

Website:_____

Username:_____

Password:_____

Notes:_____

_____

_____

Date:_____

Website:_____

Username:_____

Password:_____

Notes:_____

_____

_____

Date:_____

Website:_____

Username:_____

Password:_____

Notes:_____

_____

_____

Date:_____

Website:_____

Username:_____

Password:_____

Notes:_____

_____

_____

Date:_____

Website:_____

Username:_____

Password:_____

Notes:_____

_____

_____

Date:_____

Website:_____

Username:_____

Password:_____

Notes:_____

_____

_____

Date:_____

Website:_____

Username:_____

Password:_____

Notes:_____

_____

_____

Date:_____

Website:_____

Username:_____

Password:_____

Notes:_____

_____

_____

Date:_____

Website:_____

Username:_____

Password:_____

Notes:_____

_____

_____

Date:_____

Website:_____

Username:_____

Password:_____

Notes:_____

_____

_____

Date:_____

Website:_____

Username:_____

Password:_____

Notes:_____

_____

_____

Date:_____

Website:_____

Username:_____

Password:_____

Notes:_____

_____

_____

Date:_____

Website:_____

Username:_____

Password:_____

Notes:_____

_____

_____

Date:_____

Website:_____

Username:_____

Password:_____

Notes:_____

_____

_____

Date:_____

Website:_____

Username:_____

Password:_____

Notes:_____

_____

_____

Date:_____

Website:_____

Username:_____

Password:_____

Notes:_____

_____

_____

Date:_____

Website:_____

Username:_____

Password:_____

Notes:_____

_____

_____

Date:_____

Website:_____

Username:_____

Password:_____

Notes:_____

_____

_____

Date:_____

Website:_____

Username:_____

Password:_____

Notes:_____

_____

_____

Date:_____

Website:_____

Username:_____

Password:_____

Notes:_____

_____

_____

Date:_____

Website:_____

Username:_____

Password:_____

Notes:_____

_____

_____

Date:_____

Website:_____

Username:_____

Password:_____

Notes:_____

_____

_____

Date:_____

Website:_____

Username:_____

Password:_____

Notes:_____

_____

_____

Date:_____

Website:_____

Username:_____

Password:_____

Notes:_____

_____

_____

Date:_____

Website:_____

Username:_____

Password:_____

Notes:_____

_____

_____

Date:_____

Website:_____

Username:_____

Password:_____

Notes:_____

_____

_____

Date:_____

Website:_____

Username:_____

Password:_____

Notes:_____

_____

_____

Date:_____

Website:_____

Username:_____

Password:_____

Notes:_____

_____

_____

Date:_____

Website:_____

Username:_____

Password:_____

Notes:_____

_____

_____

Date:_____

Website:_____

Username:_____

Password:_____

Notes:_____

_____

_____

Date:_____

Website:_____

Username:_____

Password:_____

Notes:_____

_____

_____

Date:_____

Website:_____

Username:_____

Password:_____

Notes:_____

_____

_____

Date:_____

Website:_____

Username:_____

Password:_____

Notes:_____

_____

_____

Date:_____

Website:_____

Username:_____

Password:_____

Notes:_____

_____

_____

Date:_____

Website:_____

Username:_____

Password:_____

Notes:_____

_____

_____

Date:_____

Website:_____

Username:_____

Password:_____

Notes:_____

_____

_____

Date:_____

Website:_____

Username:_____

Password:_____

Notes:_____

_____

_____

Date:_____

Website:_____

Username:_____

Password:_____

Notes:_____

_____

_____

Date:_____

Website:_____

Username:_____

Password:_____

Notes:_____

_____

_____

Date:_____

Website:_____

Username:_____

Password:_____

Notes:_____

_____

_____

Date:_____

Website:_____

Username:_____

Password:_____

Notes:_____

_____

_____

Date:_____

Website:_____

Username:_____

Password:_____

Notes:_____

_____

_____

Date:_____

Website:_____

Username:_____

Password:_____

Notes:_____

_____

_____

Date:_____

Website:_____

Username:_____

Password:_____

Notes:_____

_____

_____

Date:_____

Website:_____

Username:_____

Password:_____

Notes:_____

_____

_____

Date:_____

Website:_____

Username:_____

Password:_____

Notes:_____

_____

_____

Date:_____

Website:_____

Username:_____

Password:_____

Notes:_____

_____

_____

Date:_____

Website:_____

Username:_____

Password:_____

Notes:_____

_____

_____

Date:_____

Website:_____

Username:_____

Password:_____

Notes:_____

_____

_____

Date:_____

Website:_____

Username:_____

Password:_____

Notes:_____

_____

_____

Date:_____

Website:_____

Username:_____

Password:_____

Notes:_____

_____

_____

Date:_____

Website:_____

Username:_____

Password:_____

Notes:_____

_____

_____

Date:_____

Website:_____

Username:_____

Password:_____

Notes:_____

_____

_____

Date:_____

Website:_____

Username:_____

Password:_____

Notes:_____

_____

_____

Date:_____

Website:_____

Username:_____

Password:_____

Notes:_____

_____

_____

Date:_____

Website:_____

Username:_____

Password:_____

Notes:_____

_____

_____

Date:_____

Website:_____

Username:_____

Password:_____

Notes:_____

_____

_____

Date:_____

Website:_____

Username:_____

Password:_____

Notes:_____

_____

_____

Date:_____

Website:_____

Username:_____

Password:_____

Notes:_____

_____

_____

Date:_____

Website:_____

Username:_____

Password:_____

Notes:_____

_____

_____

Date:_____

Website:_____

Username:_____

Password:_____

Notes:_____

_____

_____

Date:_____

Website:_____

Username:_____

Password:_____

Notes:_____

_____

_____

Date:_____

Website:_____

Username:_____

Password:_____

Notes:_____

_____

_____

Date:_____

Website:_____

Username:_____

Password:_____

Notes:_____

_____

_____

Date:_____

Website:_____

Username:_____

Password:_____

Notes:_____

_____

_____

Date:_____

Website:_____

Username:_____

Password:_____

Notes:_____

_____

_____

Date:_____

Website:_____

Username:_____

Password:_____

Notes:_____

_____

_____

Date:_____

Website:_____

Username:_____

Password:_____

Notes:_____

_____

_____

Date:_____

Website:_____

Username:_____

Password:_____

Notes:_____

_____

_____

Date:_____

Website:_____

Username:_____

Password:_____

Notes:_____

_____

_____

Date:_____

Website:_____

Username:_____

Password:_____

Notes:_____

_____

_____

Date:_____

Website:_____

Username:_____

Password:_____

Notes:_____

_____

_____

Date:_____

Website:_____

Username:_____

Password:_____

Notes:_____

_____

_____

Date:_____

Website:_____

Username:_____

Password:_____

Notes:_____

_____

_____

Date:_____

Website:_____

Username:_____

Password:_____

Notes:_____

_____

_____

Date:_____

Website:_____

Username:_____

Password:_____

Notes:_____

_____

_____

Date:_____

Website:_____

Username:_____

Password:_____

Notes:_____

_____

_____

Date:_____

Website:_____

Username:_____

Password:_____

Notes:_____

_____

_____

Date:_____

Website:_____

Username:_____

Password:_____

Notes:_____

_____

_____

Date:_____

Website:_____

Username:_____

Password:_____

Notes:_____

_____

_____

Date:_____

Website:_____

Username:_____

Password:_____

Notes:_____

_____

_____

Date:_____

Website:_____

Username:_____

Password:_____

Notes:_____

_____

_____

Date:_____

Website:_____

Username:_____

Password:_____

Notes:_____

_____

_____

Date:_____

Website:_____

Username:_____

Password:_____

Notes:_____

_____

_____

Date:_____

Website:_____

Username:_____

Password:_____

Notes:_____

_____

_____

Date:_____

Website:_____

Username:_____

Password:_____

Notes:_____

_____

_____

Date:_____

Website:_____

Username:_____

Password:_____

Notes:_____

_____

_____

Date:_____

Website:_____

Username:_____

Password:_____

Notes:_____

_____

_____

Date:_____

Website:_____

Username:_____

Password:_____

Notes:_____

_____

_____

Date:_____

Website:_____

Username:_____

Password:_____

Notes:_____

_____

_____

Date:_____

Website:_____

Username:_____

Password:_____

Notes:_____

_____

_____

Date:_____

Website:_____

Username:_____

Password:_____

Notes:_____

_____

_____

Date:_____

Website:_____

Username:_____

Password:_____

Notes:_____

_____

_____

Date:_____

Website:_____

Username:_____

Password:_____

Notes:_____

_____

_____

Date:_____

Website:_____

Username:_____

Password:_____

Notes:_____

_____

_____

Date:_____

Website:_____

Username:_____

Password:_____

Notes:_____

_____

_____

Date:_____

Website:_____

Username:_____

Password:_____

Notes:_____

_____

_____

Date:_____

Website:_____

Username:_____

Password:_____

Notes:_____

_____

_____

Date:_____

Website:_____

Username:_____

Password:_____

Notes:_____

_____

_____

Date:_____

Website:_____

Username:_____

Password:_____

Notes:_____

_____

_____

Date:_____

Website:_____

Username:_____

Password:_____

Notes:_____

_____

_____

Date:_____

Website:_____

Username:_____

Password:_____

Notes:_____

_____

_____

Date:_____

Website:_____

Username:_____

Password:_____

Notes:_____

_____

_____

Date:_____

Website:_____

Username:_____

Password:_____

Notes:_____

_____

_____

Date:_____

Website:_____

Username:_____

Password:_____

Notes:_____

_____

_____

Date:_____

Website:_____

Username:_____

Password:_____

Notes:_____

_____

_____

Date:_____

Website:_____

Username:_____

Password:_____

Notes:_____

_____

_____

Date:_____

Website:_____

Username:_____

Password:_____

Notes:_____

_____

_____

Date:_____

Website:_____

Username:_____

Password:_____

Notes:_____

_____

_____

Date:_____

Website:_____

Username:_____

Password:_____

Notes:_____

_____

_____

Date:_____

Website:_____

Username:_____

Password:_____

Notes:_____

_____

_____

Date:_____

Website:_____

Username:_____

Password:_____

Notes:_____

_____

_____

Date:_____

Website:_____

Username:_____

Password:_____

Notes:_____

_____

_____

Date:_____

Website:_____

Username:_____

Password:_____

Notes:_____

_____

_____

Date:_____

Website:_____

Username:_____

Password:_____

Notes:_____

_____

_____

Date:_____

Website:_____

Username:_____

Password:_____

Notes:_____

_____

_____

Date:_____

Website:_____

Username:_____

Password:_____

Notes:_____

_____

_____

Date:_____

Website:_____

Username:_____

Password:_____

Notes:_____

_____

_____

Date:_____

Website:_____

Username:_____

Password:_____

Notes:_____

_____

_____

Date:_____

Website:_____

Username:_____

Password:_____

Notes:_____

_____

_____

Date:_____

Website:_____

Username:_____

Password:_____

Notes:_____

_____

_____

Date:_____

Website:_____

Username:_____

Password:_____

Notes:_____

_____

_____

Date:_____

Website:_____

Username:_____

Password:_____

Notes:_____

_____

_____

Date:_____

Website:_____

Username:_____

Password:_____

Notes:_____

_____

_____

Date:_____

Website:_____

Username:_____

Password:_____

Notes:_____

_____

_____

Date:_____

Website:_____

Username:_____

Password:_____

Notes:_____

_____

_____

Date:_____

Website:_____

Username:_____

Password:_____

Notes:_____

_____

_____

Date:_____

Website:_____

Username:_____

Password:_____

Notes:_____

_____

_____

Date:_____

Website:_____

Username:_____

Password:_____

Notes:_____

_____

_____

Date:_____

Website:_____

Username:_____

Password:_____

Notes:_____

_____

_____

Date:_____

Website:_____

Username:_____

Password:_____

Notes:_____

_____

_____

Date:_____

Website:_____

Username:_____

Password:_____

Notes:_____

_____

_____

Date:_____

Website:_____

Username:_____

Password:_____

Notes:_____

_____

_____

Date:_____

Website:_____

Username:_____

Password:_____

Notes:_____

_____

_____

Date:_____

Website:_____

Username:_____

Password:_____

Notes:_____

_____

_____

Date:_____

Website:_____

Username:_____

Password:_____

Notes:_____

_____

_____

Date:_____

Website:_____

Username:_____

Password:_____

Notes:_____

_____

_____

Date:_____

Website:_____

Username:_____

Password:_____

Notes:_____

_____

_____

Date:_____

Website:_____

Username:_____

Password:_____

Notes:_____

_____

_____

Date:_____

Website:_____

Username:_____

Password:_____

Notes:_____

_____

_____

Date:_____

Website:_____

Username:_____

Password:_____

Notes:_____

_____

_____

Date:_____

Website:_____

Username:_____

Password:_____

Notes:_____

_____

_____

Date:_____

Website:_____

Username:_____

Password:_____

Notes:_____

_____

_____

Date:_____

Website:_____

Username:_____

Password:_____

Notes:_____

_____

_____

Date:_____

Website:_____

Username:_____

Password:_____

Notes:_____

_____

_____

Date:_____

Website:_____

Username:_____

Password:_____

Notes:_____

_____

_____

Date:_____

Website:_____

Username:_____

Password:_____

Notes:_____

_____

_____

Date:_____

Website:_____

Username:_____

Password:_____

Notes:_____

_____

_____

Date:_____

Website:_____

Username:_____

Password:_____

Notes:_____

_____

_____

Date:_____

Website:_____

Username:_____

Password:_____

Notes:_____

_____

_____

Date:_____

Website:_____

Username:_____

Password:_____

Notes:_____

_____

_____

Date:_____

Website:_____

Username:_____

Password:_____

Notes:_____

_____

_____

Date:_____

Website:_____

Username:_____

Password:_____

Notes:_____

_____

_____

Date:_____

Website:_____

Username:_____

Password:_____

Notes:_____

_____

_____

Date:_____

Website:_____

Username:_____

Password:_____

Notes:_____

_____

_____

Date:_____

Website:_____

Username:_____

Password:_____

Notes:_____

_____

_____

Date:_____

Website:_____

Username:_____

Password:_____

Notes:_____

_____

_____

Date:_____

Website:_____

Username:_____

Password:_____

Notes:_____

_____

_____

Date:_____

Website:_____

Username:_____

Password:_____

Notes:_____

_____

_____

Date:_____

Website:_____

Username:_____

Password:_____

Notes:_____

_____

_____

Date:_____

Website:_____

Username:_____

Password:_____

Notes:_____

_____

_____

Date:_____

Website:_____

Username:_____

Password:_____

Notes:_____

_____

_____

Date:_____

Website:_____

Username:_____

Password:_____

Notes:_____

_____

_____

Date:_____

Website:_____

Username:_____

Password:_____

Notes:_____

_____

_____

Date:_____

Website:_____

Username:_____

Password:_____

Notes:_____

_____

_____

Date:_____

Website:_____

Username:_____

Password:_____

Notes:_____

_____

_____

Date:_____

Website:_____

Username:_____

Password:_____

Notes:_____

_____

_____

Date:_____

Website:_____

Username:_____

Password:_____

Notes:_____

_____

_____

Date:_____

Website:_____

Username:_____

Password:_____

Notes:_____

_____

_____